# Millennium Kopprasch Series
# Rhythm Kopprasch

## Volume I

Jeffrey Agrell

Published by Wildwind Editions
Cover art by Karin Wittig
Layout and formatting by Awadhesh Yadav

First Printing: 2018


ISBN-13: 978-1719149389
ISBN-10: 1719149380

# Books by Jeffrey Agrell

*Horn Technique*

*The Creative Hornist*

*Improvisation Games for Classical Musicians (2008)*

*Improvisation Games for Classical Musicians
Vol. II (2016)*

*Improvised Chamber Music for Classical Musicians*

*Improv Games for One Player*

*Improv Duets for Classical Musicians*

*Vocal Improvisation Games
(with co-author Patrice Madura)*

*Creative Pedagogy for Piano Teachers
(with co-author Aura Strohschein)*

# The Millennium Kopprasch Series

I know what you're thinking: What? Messing with Kopprasch? Why? Is that even legal? Please explain!

I'm glad you asked those questions. What we familiarly and simply call"Kopprasch" refers to the etude collection of 60 studies for low horn Op. 6 by German composer Georg Kopprasch (ca. 1800-c. 1850). Kopprasch was a professional hornist whose career included playing in the Royal Berlin Theater Orchestra (after 1822) and the court orchestra of the Prince of Dessau (after 1832). His sixty etudes (published in two volumes) were some of the earliest etudes published for the newly invented valve horn, and are still arguably the most popular etudes for horn (as well as being regularly poached by other brasses) today.

The etudes are often quite "mechanical" in nature (with a couple of exceptions), and are essentially various elaborations of the most basic musical material: scales and arpeggios. All well and good, and still useful today, but there is one inescapable problem: a few things have changed in both the real and the musical world since the early 19th century. It goes without saying (so we will say it): the musician of the new millennium can expect to face technical and musical challenges that far exceed the basics covered by Kopprasch.

What we do in The Millennium Kopprasch Series is to take the familiar and stretch it, that is, we take Kopprasch's etudes and dramatically extend them in various ways(through this series) so that the millennium musician acquires the depth and breadth they need to survive and thrive almost two hundred years after those first original etudes were written. Look around: how many things do you see are the same as they were in 1830? Transportation. Food. Science. Communication. Clothing. Musical styles. Medicine. Sports. Anything electric. And on and on. It requires no great pains to see the tremendous differences. Hence this series, which simply asks: shouldn't musical studies reflect the demands of the current era?

The Millennium Kopprasch Series will (theoretically) eventually comprise about ten two-volume sets of revised/updated Kopprasch (heretofore our shorthand term for the etude collection), always in two volumes for each version to mirror the originals. Rhythm Kopprasch is the first. Subsequent volumes will appear every few months for the next several years. Stay tuned, and be the first on your block to collect the entire series!

*PS: send us your email address if you would like to be informed when the next set is published:* jeffrey.agrell@gmail.com

# Rhythm Kopprasch:
# Study and Performance Tips

Following are some ideas for the most efficient practice and maximum rewards from working on Rhythm Kopprasch:

- Note that no tempo markings are given. This is because tempo is the *last* element that should be worked on. It is too easy to consider the indicated tempo as the first (and perhaps final) to take. What is important is *success*, and that means starting at a very user-friendly slower tempo, in most cases. Thus: pick a tempo that works for you, right away.

- Note that not every original Kopprasch etude is used/included in Rhythm Kopprasch. This is because not every etude lent itself to rhythmic transformation. Note also that there are a few minor note (pitch) changes to accommodate the focus on rhythm of these etudes.

- Play everything at a variety of tempos, over time. Start with slow tempos. Work up to ever-faster tempos. Speed will come easily and naturally with mastery, and mastery comes from a large quantity of quality study.

- Play everything accompanied by a robust metronome click. Beware of what sometimes happens: playing *at the same time* as the metronome, but not giving complete attention to playing *exactly in time* with the click.

- Sing every etude first to work on rhythms. Singing the pitch is a nice bonus, but most important is solving all rhythm challenges before you play a note. Don't waste your chops if you can't first sing all the rhythms. Try clapping the beat while you sing the rhythms. Conquer the rhythms singing, and only after that with the instrument.

- Master small sections of each etude first. A measure or less is an excellent unit to work on. Playing through the whole etude is a great way to review all the details that you have previously worked out, but unless you are treating it as a one-time-straight-through sight reading exercise, it only serves to practice mistakes.

- Partner up. It's easier to show up and do workouts at the gym if you have a workout partner. The same goes here. Both of you sing the line in unison while clapping the beat. Then have your partner clap the beat while you play the line. Switch!.Other ideas: have one of you turn the volume metronome click off and on (if the click comes from an app) to see if the other person can keep a steady beat as the click comes and goes (i.e. the beat is still there, but is sometimes silent). Another option: instead of clapping, have one partner drum the beat (on a hand drum, table, book, piano lid, etc.).

- Metronome games. There are many possible ways to use the metronome. One is to *hear* the click on the offbeats (2 & 4). Advanced players can try hearing it on the "and" of the beat – the second 8th note. Another way is to have it click only one beat per measure (e.g. only on 1. Or 2. Or 3. Or 4).

- When you are farther down the line in mastering all the rhythm and pitch considerations of these Rhythm Kopprasch etudes, switch to some rhythm accompaniments that are more complex than the bare-bones metronome click. See **Metronomology.**

## For Further Study

As useful and effective as the study of these Rhythm Kopprasch etudes is, the study of rhythm is a very deep well, and RK just scratches the surfaces. What's next for those seeking to learn more? There are many possibilities; here are a few ideas to get you started.

- Dance. Any rhythmic body movement is a great plus in achieving a better sense of rhythm and time.

- Drum. Having a djembe or a conga drum or two is a wonderful addition to your personal musical family, but you don't need a drum to drum. Turn any available surface into a percussion instrument and enjoy the wonderful feeling of creating rhythms with your hands. Table. Desktop. Book. Lap. Dog (gently, gently). Pots and pans. Cardboard boxes. It's easy: just start. Alternate hands. Add accents, regular and irregular, duple, triple. Provide a rhythmic accompaniment to any kind of music that you like to listen to. Even with TV: drum during the commercials. Make it a duet. Drum all the time. Make percussive beats all the time, everywhere. Clap your hands, snap your fingers. Make mouth noises. Shuffle your feet. Step the big beats, tap the little beats as you walk. Create ostinatos. Take wild solos. Maybe even buy a real drum someday. But start now. Today. Right now!

- Read 1. Alan Dworsky and Betsy Sansby have created a wonderful series of tutorial books and DVDs on drumming and rhythm: see dancinghands.com

- Read 2. There are hundreds of rhythm games described in my books on classical improv games. *Improvisation Games for Classical Musicians* (2008) includes 79 rhythm games, same title, Vol. II (2016) adds 76 more. Available from booksellers or from the publisher GIA (giamusic.com).

# Metronomology

As classical musicians, we are extremely pitch-centric in everything we do. Get the note. Don't miss the note. Pick up whatever rhythm you can along the way, but don't make a (pitch) mistake! Rhythm Kopprasch presents a great opportunity to tip the balance back a bit in the direction of the most basic element of music: rhythm. However, ink on paper is not enough. To get the job done right, you must make use of a metronome (in some form) *all the time* (pun intended) as you work on these etudes (and everything else, for that matter). Electronic hardware metronomes are useful; smartphone app metronomes are much more versatile and often significantly cheaper.

## Using the Metronome

Your first task in the use of a time reminder like the simple metronome is **awareness** – of exactly where the beat/pulse is at all times, by listening – really listening – to the click as you play. The opposite of this is playing more or less independently of the click, a.k.a. playing something while sitting near a metronome. Don't laugh: this happens far too often. Our tradition is to worry mostly about pitch accuracy and not so much rhythmic precision. The common cold of classical study is a dim awareness of rhythm/pulse/beat, and thus only a very superficial rhythmic sense. We really need the aid of this rhythm police to keep us honest.

As you play, listen to the click/pulse and compare what you are playing to it on *every beat*, every single note, and make adjustments, however micro. Challenge yourself. Can you play one note per click *exactly* on the beat? Can you do this from very slow to very fast? Can you stay glued to the beat with only two clicks per measure? One? One every other measure? The process is simple, but you actually have to do it: 1. Listen. 2. Correct. 3. Repeat.

Our final goal is to develop an *internal* sense of time so that we are at last much less dependent on the *external* beat of the metronome. This is called *inchronation,* the same way that a sense of correct pitch is called intonation.

## Hardware Metronomes

A metronome is an absolute necessity. There are many choices, both hardware and software. Not recommended: the old-fashioned wind-up metal arm metronomes. They are better than nothing; they are quaint and rustically appealing in looks, but their drawback is imprecision. Below are a few samples of available electronic metronomes (there are many out there — go sample others and compare!).

### Simpler, cheaper models

Korg MA-1 — Visual Beat Counting Metronome
Korg TM50BK — tuner + metronome
Seiko SQ50–V metronome

### Middlin'

Boss DB-30C Dr. Beat Metronome
Intelli IMT301 — Five in One: digital Metronome, Tuner, Pitch Pipe, Thermo-Hygro Meter — Adjustable volume.
Korg KDM-2 — True Tone Advanced Digital Metronome

### More features, more expensive:

BOSS DB-90 — 4 kinds of clicks. Drum machine rhythms. Headphone jack. MIDI connections. Rhythm Coach (onboard mic), and more.

## Metronome Apps

There are many metronome apps that you can download to your smartphone; only a few are suggested below. Most such apps are loaded with features; they all do much more than just click the beat, but they are all very cheap compared to hardware metronomes.

**Metronomics.** Besides the main beat, you may add up to 3 more beat subdivisions, and you can select how often that subdivision will drop out (be silent). You can choose to hear the downbeat every (you choose the number) of bars how often to repeat each bar (perhaps repeating a pattern), and if you want a bar to be silent and how often. You can also save, store, and share your settings and patterns.

**Time Guru.** Simple, elegant layout. Select a meter by hitting one of the numbers 1-7 at the top. Then you can randomly mute (by %) when the beat sounds — if the beat is silent sometimes, you are forced to be more accurate.

**PolyNome.** Probably the top metronome app for complex rhythms. Originally developed to help players transition between note values, e.g. 16ths to triplets and how to play polyrhythms. You can add silent bars to the click, create any polyrhythm combination from 1 to 32. If you get a little deeper into it, you can create interesting percussion grooves. There is a "PolyNome Public Library" where other users share their grooves and patterns.

**Tonal Energy Tuner& Metronome.** Popular tuner + metronome practice aid. Attractive visual displays. Audio/visual recording features. Bluetooth and many other features.

**TempoPerfect Metronome.** Free software download.

> You will need to either play any of these through speakers, or – easier – through ear buds. The ear buds are probably better because you can hear both the click sounds and the horn; sometimes the horn volume covers up the sound from a speaker.

## Drum Machine Apps

For those interested in greater challenge and rhythmic variety. These can serve as metronomes, but are designed to provide interesting (read: challenging) rhythm accompaniment. They are much more challenging to play with than a basic metronome click because of their more complex rhythms. They are more expensive than basic metronome apps, but compared to hardware drum machines they are still a bargain. Note: check YouTube.com and Google for free video tutorials on how to use these apps.

Current favorites:

**AfroLatin DM.** Many, many Afro-Latin rhythms, including *son clave,* guaguanco, bembe, mambo, merengue, and 100 more. You can edit or create your own rhythms.

**Brazilian DM.** By the same people (lumbeat.com) who made AfroLatin DM. Similar features using Brazilian rhythms. More challenging aurally than the AfroLatin.

**Rock Drum Machine.** Rock drum set rhythms.

**SuperMetronome Groovebox Pro**. Jazz/rock drum set rhythms.

**Compás Flamenco.** A kind of metronome that displays and counts the most common flamenco clapping rhythms (e.g. *soleá, bulerias,* etc.).s

**iTabla Pro.** The most complex of the lot, but a great source for the sounds and rhythms of Indian (Hindustani) music.

## Wait, There's More

In Volume II of Rhythm Kopprasch (in preparation as Vol. I is published), there will be more metronome information and activities, including Rhythm Warm-Ups and metronome games.

# Millennium Kopprasch Series

# Rhythm Kopprasch

## Volume I

Jeffrey Agrell

# K1

Rhythm elements: triplets, ties, syncopation

# K2

Rhythm elements: duple vs triple, triplets, ties, syncopation.

# K3

Rhythm elements: odd meters, meter changes, accents

# K4

Rhythm elements: 16ths, ties, syncopation

# K5

Rhythm elements: beat subdivision, syncopation

All done using C horn (= F:13 fingering), i.e. overtones
Repeat all in Db horn (F:23), D horn (F:12), Eb horn (F:1), E horn (F:2), and F horn (F:0)

# K6

Rhythm elements: triplets and quintuplets, duple vs triple, articulation

# K7

Rhythm elements: ties, triplets, meter change, duple vs triple

# K8

Rhythm elements: odd meters, meter change, 16ths

# K9

Rhythm elements: syncopation, meters (4/4, 3/8, 4/8, 5/8, 6/8, 3/4) accents, duple vs triple, 4 over 3, 3 over 2

# K10

Rhythm elements: syncopation, 16ths, ties

[K11: omitted]

# K12

Rhythm elements: 5 over 4, 3 over 2, 5 over 2, clave beat (3+3+2), ties, syncopation, triple/duple

[NB: these are *not* triplets]

# K13

Rhythm elements: meters (4/8, 5/8, 6/8, 7/8, 2/4, 3/4), accents

# K14

Rhythm elements: duple/triple/quintuple, ties, syncopation, 5/4 meter, rests

[K15 omitted]

# K16

Rhythm elements: meters (3/16, 5/16, 6/16, 8/16), clave rhythm

# K17

Rhythm elements: syncopation, ties, 16ths, quintuplets (5 over 4)

14

# K18

Rhythm elements: rests, 3/4 vs 6/8 meters

# K19

Rhythm elements: meters (3/8, 4/8, 5/8, 7/8), ties, rests

# K20

Rhythm elements: clave rhythm (3+3+2), ties, rests,

# K21

Rhythm elements: meters (3/4, 6/8, 4/4, 5/8), ties, syncopation, triplets, clave rhythm

[K22 is omitted]

# K23

Rhythm elements: syncopation, ties

# K24

Rhythm elements: meters (5/16, 6/16, 7/16, 9/16)

# K25

Rhythm elements: swing 8ths, rests, accents, ties

# K26

Rhythm elements: tuplets: triplets, 3 over 2, 3 over 4, 5 over 2, 5 over 4

# K27

Rhythm elements: meters (12/8, 11/8, 10/8, 9/8)

25

# K28

Rhythm elements: dotted rhythms in 6/8

# K29

Rhythm elements: ties, meters (3/8, 2/4), 3 over 2

# K30

Rhythm elements: ties, triplets, meters (4/4, 5/4, 5/8), rests

# K31

Rhythm elements: meters (6/8, 7/8, 2/4), ties

(K32 & K33 omitted)

# K34

Rhythm elements: meters (6/16, 9/16, 8/8 [clave: 3+3+2])

# About the Author

**Jeffrey Agrell** has earned his living playing and teaching horn since college. After a first career as a symphony orchestra musician, he has been horn professor at the University of Iowa since 2000.

He has performed and taught the full gamut of horn literature, including the repertoire for symphony orchestra, opera, musicals, ballet, operetta, and chamber music, while stretching personal artistic boundaries beyond the orchestra as a educator, composer, writer, clinician, recording artist, and solo performer. He is a former two-term member of the Advisory Council of the International Horn Society, has been a member of the faculty of the Asian Youth Orchestra in Hong Kong, and has taught at the prestigious Kendall Betts Horn Camp since 2005.

Besides performing, he has won awards as both a writer and composer, with well over one hundred published articles and nine books to his credit, most recently, *Horn Technique* (447 p., 2017) and *The Creative Hornist* (228 p., 2017). He is an expert on classical improvisation, and has authored landmark books in this area, including *Improvisation Games for Classical Musicians,* Vol. I (2008) and Vol. II (2016).

Outside of horn and writing, he is a used-to-be amateur jazz guitarist, and currently an enthusiastic, if not particularly skilled conga drum player.

To contact Jeffrey Agrell with questions, comments, crazy ideas, get into interesting discussions about any of this, or engage him for concerts, workshops, keynote addresses, masterclasses, and all that, write to him at jeffrey.agrell@gmail.com

Made in the USA
Middletown, DE
26 August 2022

71363711R00031